Christingle Playlets

(Suitable for Schools, Junior Church,
Sunday Schools etc)

by
Jackie Marchant

British Library Cataloguing in Publication Data.
A catalogue record for this book is available
from the British Library.

ISBN 086071 582 5

MOORLEY'S Print & Publishing
23 Park Rd., Ilkeston, Derbys DE7 5DA
Tel/Fax: (0115) 932 0643

The Tradition of Christingle

The custom of the Christingle began in the Moravian Church and was first used as part of a Christmas Children's Festival in the Marienborn Congregation in Germany on the 24th December 1747; this service was conducted by Bishop John de Watteville.

After the congregation had sung some hymns, he read some verses which the children themselves had written 'in honour of the Saviour's birth'. He then explained that happiness had come from the birth of Jesus 'who has kindled in each little heart a flame which keeps ever burning to their joy and our happiness'. To make the point even clearer each child then received a little lighted wax candle with a red ribbon. John de Watteville ended the service with his prayer:

'Lord Jesus, kindle a flame in these dear children's hearts, that theirs like thine become.'

The Marienborn Diary concludes, 'hereupon the children went full of joy with their little lighted candles to their rooms and so went glad and happy to bed'.

No one knows for certain when the word "Christingle" was first used or from what it derived, but wherever the Moravians went in the great outreach of missionary evangelism in the 18th and 19th centuries they took with them the custom of the Christingle.

The symbolism gradually developed and today in Britain the Christingle consists of an orange representing the world, with four cocktail sticks on which are impaled nuts and raisins representing the four seasons of the year and the fruits of the earth. Around the orange is a red ribbon or tape representing the blood of Christ and the salvation of the world. The orange is surmounted by a candle symbolising Christ the Light of the world.

In Moravian churches the Christingle service is usually held on the Sunday before Christmas or on Christmas Eve and sometimes on Christmas Day. Essentially it is a children's celebration of the Christ-child which reaches its climax when each child receives their lighted candle or Christingle in the darkened church, symbolising the truth of the Christmas story that in the world's darkness there has shined a great light.

The tradition has now been taken up by most of the Christian denominations and has become a major fund-raising initiative for the Children's Society.

The Bad Apple

Characters
Narrator/s (alternatively use one narrator and give children speaking parts)

An Orange

Some Apples

Girl and Boy (dressed up as Mary and Joseph)

Other Nativity characters

If using narrators, actions are mimed

Props
A large, red ribbon; a model of a stick with sweets on; a model of a candle

Setting
A room in a house (no props needed)

Several apples surround 1 orange

Narrator   It was Christmas time again and the apples were very cross. (*Apples put hands on hips and look cross*). First of all they had been moved from their special place in the middle of the table and onto the sideboard. This always happened at Christmas, to make room for the special table decoration. Then, even worse, that **thing** (*apples turn to glare at orange*) had been put right in the middle of their bowl. It was truly dreadful. They didn't have the best spot in the room any more. But that was nothing to having to share their precious bowl with the most ugly, disgustingly smelly thing. Soon, the apples began to complain.

Narrator "Ugh!" they said (*apples hold noses*) "what's that horrible smell! I think it's coming from the middle of the bowl. It's spoiling our own lovely perfume."

Narrator "Look at its horrible skin! (*apples point at orange*) It's not normal. It's all bumpy, not lovely and smooth like ours."

Narrator "And what a colour! (*Apples frown*) Apples are supposed to be red or green. That apple is a different colour. I don't like it."

Narrator "Neither do I. That's a **bad** apple." (*hands on hips*)

Narrator The apples all agreed, that the bad apple in the middle of the bowl was not to be trusted. You couldn't trust an apple with a funny smell. You couldn't trust an apple with bumpy skin. You couldn't trust an apple that was the wrong colour. The other apples refused to have anything to do with the bad apple in the middle of their bowl. (*Apples fold arms and turn away from orange*) The bad apple was very, very sad. (*Orange looks sad*)

Narrator	"I can't help it," the bad apple said to itself, "I was just born like this. I've always had this smell and this bumpy, strange coloured skin. Oh I wish I wasn't so ugly! I wish I was the same as all the other apples, so they would like me." But the other apples ignored the bad apple and just carried on talking as though it wasn't there.
	(*Enter children dressed as Mary and Joseph. They stand in front of the apples and orange.*)
Narrator	The apples became very excited. The children had come in and were looking at their bowl. They thought they were going to be put back on their special place in the middle of the table again. But the children didn't pick them up. Instead, they took the bad apple. They took it out of the bowl and put it on the table, right in the middle. In the apples' special place! (*Children lead orange to front. Apples put hands on hips and look cross*)
Narrator	The girl, who was dressed as Mary, spoke to the bad apple, "You are very important," she said. "We want you to be in this special spot in the middle of the table, while we practise our nativity play. After that, we're going to take you to church with us for the Christingle Service."

Narrator	The apples were furious. They began to shout and complain. (*apples mime shouting and wagging fingers*) But, suddenly, they stopped. The children were doing very strange things to the bad apple.
Narrator	"Now," they said, "you are a very special **orange**. (*Apples turn to look, open mouthed, at children and orange. Orange looks puzzled*). You are the world, created by God."
Narrator	"And here is a red ribbon for you," they said and tied a beautiful red ribbon around the orange (*girl and boy tie red ribbon round the orange's middle*) "this is the blood of Jesus, who died for us, and rose again in glory."
Narrator	They placed some sweets and nuts into the orange. (*girl hands orange a stick with sweets and nuts. Orange holds it in one hand*). "These are all the good things which God has given us," they said.
Narrator	Then they put a candle into the orange (*boy hands orange a candle*) "This is the light of Christ," they said "The light of Christ enters the whole world. It will enter our lives if we ask."
Narrator	The apples were silent. They were ashamed of themselves (*apples hang heads*). They had hated the orange just because it was different. They never gave

it a chance to prove itself. Now they knew that the orange was very special. How they wished they'd been nice to it. But when the girl and boy held the orange up, it smiled kindly at them (*boy and girl hold arms of orange up. Orange smiles at apples*). And when the girl and boy put it back in the middle of the table, the apples didn't mind at all.

| Narrator | Suddenly, the doorbell went. Lots of other children came into the room, all dressed up. (*enter nativity characters*) |

| Narrator | "Great, you've arrived!" said the girl and boy, "now we can practise our nativity play." |

| Narrator | The apples watched as Mary and Joseph came to the stable*. They watched the baby Jesus being placed in the manger*. They saw the shepherds come and bring gifts*. They saw the wise men bringing their gifts of gold, frankincense and myrrh*. They loved the pretty angels who came by the stable. And they were very happy that their new friend, the Christingle orange, was using its candle to light up the whole scene. (*Nativity characters act accordingly*). |

THE END

The Red Ribbon

Characters

Narrator/s (or use one narrator and give children speaking parts)

Reverend John (depending on denomination and local customs substitute "Father" or "Pastor")

Annie (a young girl)

Mrs Simmons the Sunday School teacher

Nativity characters

Setting
Reverend John's office at the back of church. The church.

Props
A red ribbon, an orange, candle etc for a Christingle orange

Reverend John enters his study, rubbing his hands with cold.

Narrator   Reverend John was in his office at the back of the church. His fire was lit, but it wasn't very warm. But it was much warmer than outside, where there was an icy wind and freezing snow. It was going to be a very cold Christmas this year.

Annie walks down the aisle.

Narrator	Outside, a little girl was walking in the snow. Her name was Annie. Her clothes were poor and she had no coat. Her dress was worn and faded, her shoes were in tatters and her shawl had lots of holes in. Her long hair was tied up in a pony tail.
Narrator	The pony tail was held by a beautiful red ribbon, thick and soft and so shiny that it seemed to cheer up the freezing cold air around it. Annie's red ribbon was the most precious thing she had. She wore it every day.
Narrator	Reverend John looked out of his window and saw Annie walking by, her red ribbon fluttering brightly in the chilly wind. He opened his door and asked her to come in out of the cold.
Narrator	"Where are you going on such a cold day?" he asked her. She said she was going nowhere. "What a beautiful ribbon you have in your hair," said Reverend John.
Narrator	Annie clutched her ribbon. "It's mine!" she said, frightened. "It's all I have. Please don't take it away from me!"
Narrator	"Of course I won't take it from you," said Reverend John, kindly. "Now, why don't you warm yourself up by the fire?" Annie sat by the fire and soon she felt warmer and less afraid. Reverend John sat at his desk

and began to write. "What are you doing?" asked Annie.

Narrator   "I'm writing a play about Jesus, which the children are going to perform in this church. Then I'm going to make a Christingle for the service. Would you like to help me?"

Narrator   "Who's Jesus?" asked Annie. "What's a Christingle?"

Narrator   Reverend John opened his desk drawer and took out an orange. Annie's eyes widened. She had only ever seen an orange once before. It had smelt so delicious and she'd longed to taste it, but the girl who was eating it wouldn't give her any.

Narrator   "Imagine that this orange is the world," explained Reverend John, "which was made by God." Then he took a bag out of his drawer. From the bag he pulled out some nuts and sweets and sharp sticks. Annie watched as he put the nuts and sweets onto the sticks. She had only ever tasted a nut once. And she'd never had a sweet. How she longed for one!

Narrator   "These are all the good things that God has given us," said Reverend John and stuck the sweets and nuts into the orange. Then he found a candle in his drawer and put it into the top of the orange. "This is the light of the world," he said, "the most precious gift that God has given us – Jesus Christ."

Narrator   "Jesus who?" said Annie. But before Reverend John could answer her, the door opened and an icy draught of air blew in as Mrs Simmons, the Sunday school teacher, stepped into Reverend John's study. "The children are all in church," she said. "Would you like to watch them practice their nativity play?"

Narrator   "Come with us, Annie," said Reverend John, "and I will show you who Jesus is." So Annie went with Reverend John and the Sunday School teacher into the church *(Reverend John, Annie and Mrs Simmons walk down the aisle to back of church. Nativity characters get ready)* and watched the children perform their nativity play, while Reverend John told Annie all about Jesus.

Nativity Characters perform while Narrator speaks

Narrator   "A long time ago, at Christmas time, Mary and Joseph had a baby boy, born in a stable in Bethlehem. He was so special that a shiny star came and settled over the place where he was born. He was so special, that three wise Kings travelled for miles, just to see him and bring him gifts of gold, frankincense and myrrh. He was so special, that humble shepherds came and knelt by him."

Narrator	"Why was he so special?" asked Annie. "I was born in a stable and I'm not special. In fact, that is why I'm not special."
Narrator	"Jesus was God's greatest gift to us, Annie," said Reverend John. "He grew up and taught us how to be good. And you are a special girl, because Jesus loves you."
Narrator	Annie frowned. "How do you know?"
Narrator	"Come back into my office and I will show you."

Annie and Reverend John walk back down the aisle (Nativity characters could remain where they are)

Narrator	Back in his office, Reverend John picked up the orange, which had sweets and nuts stuck in it and a candle on the top. "I have to do one more thing to this orange," said Reverend John. "You see, when he grew up, Jesus died for us. He died because he loves us. All of us, whether we are rich or poor, whether we were born in a stable or in a mansion. And that includes you, Annie."
Narrator	"So someone does love me!" said Annie and gave Reverend John the most beautiful smile he'd ever seen.
Narrator	Reverend John continued. "Now, I just need a piece of red ribbon to go round the middle of this orange."

Narrator	"What for?" said Annie.
Narrator	"This is the blood of Jesus, which he shed for us when he died on the cross," said Reverend John.
Narrator	"Because he loved us so much?" said Annie.
Narrator	"That's right," said Reverend John. "Now, if I could just find my piece of red ribbon, we could finish making this Christingle." But Reverend John couldn't find a piece of red ribbon anywhere. The only red ribbon to be found was the beautiful ribbon in Annie's hair – the most special thing she had in the whole world.
Narrator	"Oh dear," said Reverend John, "I'm not going to be able to finish making this Christingle after all."
Narrator	Very slowly and carefully, Annie took the red ribbon from her hair and gave it to Reverend John.
Narrator	"Oh no, Annie," said Reverend John. "You can't possibly give me this. I know how special it is to you.'"
Narrator	"It's the most special thing I have," said Annie, "and that is why I want to give it to you – for Jesus. Please put it round the orange." So, Reverend John put Annie's

red ribbon round the orange. When he lit the candle on top of the orange, the red ribbon shone even more and the whole of Reverend John's study lit up with light. Reverend John gave the Christingle to Annie.

Narrator   "I want you to have this," he said. "Take it with you and remember that Jesus is the light of the World. When this candle has finished burning you can eat all the things on the sticks and then you can eat the orange."

Narrator   At first Annie couldn't speak. Then she said. . .

Narrator   "That is the best gift anyone could ever give me. Thank you for helping me to find Jesus."

The End

We are growing publishers, adding several new titles to our list each year. We also undertake private publications and commissioned works.

Our range includes:-

Books of Verse:
Devotional Poetry
Recitations for Children
Humorous Monologues

Drama
Bible Plays
Sketches
Christmas, Passiontide,
    Easter and Harvest Plays
Demonstrations

Resource Books
Assembly Material
Songs and Musicals
Children's Addresses
Prayers
Worship and Preaching
Books for Speakers

Activity Books
Quizzes
Puzzles
Painting Books

Church Stationery
Notice Books
Cradle Roll Certificates
Presentation Labels

Associated Lists and Imprints
Cliff College Publishing
Nimbus Press
Headway
Social Workers Christian Fellowship

Please send a stamped addressed envelope (C5 approx 9″ x 6″) for the current catalogue or consult your local Christian Bookshop who will either stock or be able to obtain Moorleys titles.